ONLY THE LOVER SINGS

Art and Contemplation

JOSEF PIEPER

ONLY THE
LOVER SINGS

Art and Contemplation

Translated by Lothar Krauth

IGNATIUS PRESS   SAN FRANCISCO

Title of the German original:
Nur der Liebende singt
©1988 Schwabenverlag AG
Ostfildern bei Stuttgart, Germany

Cover design by Roxanne Mei Lum
Cover border by Pamela Kennedy
Calligraphy by Victoria Hoke Lane

© 1990 Ignatius Press, San Francisco
ISBN 978-0-89870-302-3
Library of Congress Catalogue Number 90–81771
Printed in the United States of America

Cantare amantis est
—St. Augustine

Reason speaks in words alone
But love has a song
—Joseph de Maistre

Dedicated to
Hilde Schürk-Frisch
Sculptor and Friend

CONTENTS

PREFACE

These meditations define a great arc, spanning the distance from Augustine's marvelously formulated insight that "only he who loves can sing" all the way to the anguished cry of Hölderlin's ode entitled "Wherefore Poets in a Time of Distress?" The intent here is to make one thing clear: that music, the fine arts, poetry—anything that festively raises up human existence and thereby constitutes its true riches—all derive their life from a hidden root, and this root is a contemplation which is turned toward God and the world so as to affirm them.

WORK, SPARE TIME, AND LEISURE

T HESE THREE CONCEPTS, at first sight, do not give any indication that they hide a deeply challenging problem, and no mere theoretical problem either. No, they rather give the impression of being entirely innocuous; they could easily be understood, approvingly or with reservations, as an invitation "to take it easy". Our title seems to project an uncomplicated, even cheerful, serenity, progressing from one concept to the next. "Work", it is true, may still be part of life's burden, but it is already alleviated and forgotten as it leads to "spare time" and finally to "leisure", with its vision of the solitary fisherman who in utter contentment sits on a summer lakeshore, less intent on catching a fish than simply on relaxing and daydreaming. Where, pray, should the problem be lurking?

The term and concept of "work" are entirely familiar to us. Work is that which gives man's workday its name; it satisfies our basic needs and procures our daily bread; it constitutes the active effort to provide those things indispensable in order to stay alive. Nothing is more obvious.

And why should the meaning of "spare time" not be equally obvious? Spare time is a multilay-

This talk was the keynote address at the opening of an art exhibition in conjunction with the *Ruhrfestspiele* (1953). First published in *Die Zeit*, June 25, 1953.

ered concept. As long as it is defined *negatively*, as a span of time *not* filled with work, no problem arises. Similarly, if we consider the concept of spare time only in its relationship to the concept of "workday", if we define spare time as a mere break from work in order to recover, a time after work to restore one's strength for more work, then again, no particular problem will arise.

But some second thought might stir us up as soon as we consider that we do not really succeed in defining spare time only in this way. A moment ago I used, in all innocence, the term "workday". The notion of workday immediately evokes one other notion, closely related, which provides a rather fresh and now positive definition of spare time—a definition indicating that here we are discussing something beyond a mere break in working time or a pause to gather new strength. This other notion is "holiday". On the one hand, we have not succeeded—rather: not yet!—in eliminating the notion of holiday from our thinking (which shows the persistence of Western tradition.) On the other hand, this notion of holiday has generally lost for us its clarity, depth, and unquestioned inner meaning (which indicates how weakened and threatened our Western standards have become). A holiday, a feast day—what is this, anyway, and what in essence does it mean?

How does the spirit of celebration originate in the heart of man, how can it be fostered and preserved? And how can we possibly observe a feast day on a truly existential level without such a spirit of celebration? I very much fear that the typical modern man may no longer be able to draw answers to these questions from immediate awareness and inner experience. Of course, we still have some vague notion that the seventh day of the week is not simply the "weekend" but has a deeper significance. We still are receptive to the reminder implied in that uniquely German term *Feierabend* [meaning, "quitting time", but literally, "evening for celebration"]—the reminder that more is meant here than a mere break to catch one's breath. And we still have not entirely forgotten that the German word *Ferien* (vacation time) literally means "festive time". All of which, taken together, means one thing: the concept of spare time is by no means so simple and innocuous as at first it may have appeared. It springs from some profound dimension where it merges, lacking precise bounds, with the third concept, that of "leisure".

About this concept we confidently dare to affirm that we do not know what it means. More to the point: we are ignorant of how the concept of "leisure" is understood in the accumulated wisdom of our Western cultural and existential tradition as expressed, say, by Plato, Aristotle, or the great teachers of Christianity. Granted, one could say: but why *should* we know that? What difference does this particular ignorance make? The way we see the human person and therefore the meaning of our existence has, after all, changed considerably since the time of antiquity and the Middle Ages!

Such an objection must not be taken lightly. At any rate, however, even should we agree with it (and then especially), we have to realize what in truth this discussion is all about. We must understand that a total and final disintegration of the concept of "leisure", a basic concept of traditional Western thinking, will have a clear historical consequence; namely, the totalitarian work state. If we dislike this consequence, we must understand that there can be only one valid objection against the idolizing of labor, an objection based on some ultimate truth about human nature and therefore of sole and lasting relevance. To identify such an objection, we must discover anew, and appropriate again, the meaning of the statement, "We work so we can have leisure."

What indeed is declared here? A veritable thicket of misconceptions must be cleared away before the true meaning of this statement can appear. For this purpose, it is indispensable to spell out certain simple basics. It seems the German language is no help in this, since *Musse* (leisure) and *Müssiggang* (loafing) distressingly are such close neighbors, though in terminology only. Looking at the factual content, "loafing" is the exact opposite of "engaging in leisure" (as the ancient Greeks put it, *scholén agein*). "We work so we can have leisure", would therefore, as a preliminary approach, declare this: we work in order to do—to enable us to do—something other than work. What is this "something other"? Recreation, entertainment, amusement, play—all this is *not* meant here. Wouldn't it be quite nonsensical to think of work as drawing its justification from play? No, this "something other" indicates an activity meaningful in itself. But is not work equally meaningful? Meaningful indeed! Yet not meaningful in itself. This precisely defines the concept of work: it has a practical purpose, it produces utilitarian goods, it contributes to the common useful wealth (and "useful" always means "good for something else"). To serve some other purpose is the essential characteristic of work. In this context also belongs the old and rather offensive expression, "servile work". The terms alone do not at all imply any contempt for work, much less for the worker. We can say the opposite is true.

But then, traditional wisdom has always understood that there are also human activities that do not serve some other purpose and so are not servile. These are forms of activities to which everybody, including the working man, is entitled, even as a fundamental right and necessity (in the same way as the servile activity, namely work, which satisfies basic needs and serves a practical purpose, is as a rule required of everybody).

At this point it seems advisable to mention the old distinction—some would say, the old-fashioned and only historically relevant distinction—between "servile arts" and "liberal arts", *artes serviles* and *artes liberales*. This distinction, in fact, is anything but old-fashioned; it can claim a contemporary political relevance. Translated into the jargon of a world defined by work alone, it says: not only do production quotas and the implementation of planning goals exist, but in addition and by right, there are human activities that by their very nature lie beyond the standards of any five-year-plan. This means that there are human actions that need not be justified by a society's yardstick of economical usefulness, and absolutely so. All we have to do is use such terms to bring out the radical challenge to the domain of absolute work. This challenge is contained in the traditional Western tenet: there do exist "liberal arts", there do exist human activities that are meaningful without being either work or mere respite (from work, for more work). This too, I hope, has become clear: it is an insidiously dangerous and consequential undertaking to deny that work is characterized by its "usefulness-for-something-else", even—yes!—by its "servile" dimension. It is a fiction to declare work, the production of useful things, to be meaningful in itself. Such fiction leads to the exact opposite of what it seems to accomplish. It brings about the exact opposite of "liberation", "elevation", or "rehabilitation" for the worker. It brings about precisely that inhuman dimension so typical of the world of absolute work: it accomplishes the final bondage of man within the process of work, it explicitly makes everybody a proletarian. This is happening openly and explicitly in those totalitarian "Workers' States", but it is also infecting all other parts of the world, at least as a danger and temptation. It shows, for instance, in the difficulty we experience in answering this question: of what, then, might such activity "meaningful in itself", such "liberal" activity, consist? How should we conceive of such an activity that does not need something other for its justification, that is not defined as producing useful goods and objective results? An activity that does not bring forth the means for our existence but is existential realization itself, an activity in which man's true and proper good, his genuine richness, fullest life, and most perfect happiness is attained?

Obviously, an answer here is possible only if a specific concept of the human person is accepted. For nothing less is at stake here than the ultimate fulfillment of human existence. We are really asking how such fulfillment may come about. Originality, or the lack of it, seems to me quite irrelevant in this regard. I am only trying to express the teaching found in the Western philosophical tradition. The most important element in this teaching declares: the ultimate fulfillment, the absolutely meaningful activity, the most perfect expression of being alive, the deepest satisfaction, and the fullest achievement of human existence must needs happen in an instance of beholding, namely in the contemplating awareness of the world's ultimate and intrinsic foundations. Thus would Plato express the sum total of his insights:

Here, if anywhere at all—so spoke the foreign maiden from Mantineia (Diotima)—here man's life becomes fully worth living; for here he beholds the divine revealed in the purity of beauty itself: through this he becomes immortal.

A rather small step will bring us back again to the realm of concrete things. The reader may al-

ready have wondered, with some misgivings or
even dismay, how many more abstruse philosophical subtleties he must endure. Fear not; we
have returned to our entirely practical question:
What constitutes, here and now, an activity meaningful in itself? I have stated it before: if we are unable to answer this question, then we will also be
unable to resist convincingly the claims of a world
absolutely defined by work. The answer contained in our Western philosophical tradition
could be summed up in this way. Whenever in reflective and receptive contemplation we touch,
even remotely, the core of all things, the hidden,
ultimate reason of the living universe, the divine
foundation of all that is, the purest form of all archetypes (and the act of perception, immersed in
contemplation, is the most intensive form of
grasping and owning), whenever and wherever
we thus behold the very essence of reality—there
is an activity that is meaningful in itself taking
place.

Such reaching out in contemplation to the root
and foundation of all that is, to the archetypes of
all things, this activity that is meaningful in itself
can happen in countless actual forms. A particularly venerable form, particularly neglected as
well, is religious meditation, the contemplative
immersion of the self into the divine mysteries.
Another form is philosophical reflection, which

should indeed not be conceived as limited to some specialized academic discipline. Anybody can ponder human deeds and happenings and thus gaze into the unfathomable depths of destiny and history; anybody can get absorbed in the contemplation of a rose or human face and thus touch the mystery of creation; everybody, therefore, participates in the quest that has stirred the minds of the great philosophers since the beginning. We see still another form of such activity in the creation of the artist, who does not so much aim at presenting copies of reality as rather making visible and tangible in speech, sound, color, and stone, the archetypical essences of all things as he was privileged to perceive them. But those, too, who experience the spark of poetry while listening to a poem, who behold a sculpture and perceive the artist's intention—yes, those who only listen and observe, as long as the conditions are right, can also touch, in contemplation, the core of all reality, the domain of the eternal archetypes. "If the conditions are right"—here lies the difficulty. It is specifically the difficulty already mentioned: to be aware of those different forms of touching the core of reality and to acknowledge them as "meaningful in themselves", to experience them and simply to live them as such. Could it be that this difficulty represents the deeper reason for the increasing isolation today surrounding artists and poets, but also philosophers and certainly those dedicated to the contemplative life?

We ought to mention here certain conditions and premises intimately tied, it seems, to the activity that is meaningful in itself. Not much more than a brief enumeration is possible, though.

An activity which is meaningful in itself, first, cannot be accomplished except with an attitude of receptive openness and attentive silence—which, indeed, is the exact opposite of the worker's attitude marked by concentrated exertion. One of the fundamental human experiences is the realization that the truly great and uplifting things in life come about perhaps not without our own efforts but nevertheless not through those efforts. Rather, we will obtain them only if we can accept them as free gifts.

With this, we touch on a second precondition, even more fundamental than the first and more removed from any willful manipulation. If this other condition is not fulfilled, we cannot expect to accomplish any action meaningful in itself. Rather, we cannot expect that the meditative perception of the world's foundations will be experienced as meaningful in itself, whether it happens in the form of poetry, music, the fine arts, philosophy, or religious contemplation. This second condition, in a nutshell, is this: the ability to celebrate a feast. What, then, is required to celebrate a feast? Obviously more than a day off from work. This requirement includes man's willing acceptance of the ultimate truth, in spite of the world's riddles, even when this truth is beheld through the veil of our own tears; it includes man's awareness of being in harmony with these fundamental realities and surrounded by them. To express such acceptance, such harmony, such unity in nonordinary ways—this has been called since time immemorial: to celebrate a feast. And at this point we realize that there can be no feast without gods; indeed, that the cultic celebration is the primordial form of any feast. This, however, is a different topic.

And yet, this much shall be stated here: only such a fundamental attitude of acceptance can create, within the flow of workdays, the liberal breathing space that allows us, oblivious of life's more basic necessities, to do what is meaningful in itself. It is for this reason, on the other hand, that all forms of "liberal" activities, above all in the area of the arts, are essentially of a festive nature as long as they contain at least some remote echo of that fundamental attitude of acceptance. Wherever this attitude becomes entirely defunct, there all endeavors to organize "relaxation" surely turn into an even more hectic, indeed an outright desperate, form of work. This is not such a farfetched notion and hardly requires concrete proof. And one further aspect, I think, is not foreign to our personal experience. It is artistic activity especially that can degenerate—either into idle and empty game playing or into some novel and sophisticated form of busy-ness, profiteering, and nervous distraction—if it does not simply sink to the level of crass entertainment apt to seduce man to make himself a prisoner of his workdays with no thought of escaping.

Wherever the arts are nourished through the festive contemplation of universal realities and their sustaining reasons, there in truth something like a liberation occurs: the stepping-out into the open under an endless sky, not only for the creative artist himself but for the beholder as well, even the most humble. Such liberation, such foreshadowing of the ultimate and perfect fulfillment, is necessary for man, almost more necessary than his daily bread, which is indeed indispensable and yet insufficient.

In this precisely do I see the meaning of that statement in Aristotle's *Nicomachean Ethics,* "We work so we can have leisure."

LEARNING HOW TO SEE AGAIN

M AN'S ABILITY TO *see* is in decline. Those who nowadays concern themselves with culture and education will experience this fact again and again. We do not mean here, of course, the physiological sensitivity of the human eye. We mean the spiritual capacity to perceive the visible reality as it truly is.

To be sure, no human being has ever really *seen* everything that lies visibly in front of his eyes. The world, including its tangible side, is unfathomable. Who would ever have perfectly perceived the countless shapes and shades of just one wave swelling and ebbing in the ocean! And yet, there are degrees of perception. Going below a certain bottom line quite obviously will endanger the integrity of man as a spiritual being. It seems that nowadays we have arrived at this bottom line.

I am writing this on my return from Canada, aboard a ship sailing from New York to Rotterdam. Most of the other passengers have spent quite some time in the United States, many for one reason only: to visit and see the New World with their own eyes. *With their own eyes:* in this lies the difficulty.

First published in the catalog for an art exhibition by the *Werkschule Münster* (1952); reprinted in *Baukunst und Werkform* (Frankfurt, Main, Nov. 1952).

During the various conversations on deck and at the dinner table I am always amazed at hearing almost without exception rather generalized statements and pronouncements that are plainly the common fare of travel guides. It turns out that hardly anybody has noticed those frequent small signs in the streets of New York that indicate public fallout shelters. And visiting New York University, who would have noticed those stone-hewn chess tables in front of it, placed in Washington Square by a caring city administration for the Italian chess enthusiasts of that area?!

Or again, at table I had mentioned those magnificent fluorescent sea creatures whirled up to the surface by the hundreds in our ship's bow wake. The next day it was casually mentioned that "last night there was nothing to be seen". Indeed, for nobody had the patience to let the eyes adapt to the darkness. To repeat, then: man's ability to *see* is in decline.

Searching for the reasons, we could point to various things: modern man's restlessness and stress, quite sufficiently denounced by now, or his total absorption and enslavement by practical goals and purposes. Yet one reason must not be overlooked either: the average person of our time loses the ability to see because *there is too much to see!*

There does exist something like "visual noise", which just like the acoustical counterpart, makes clear perception impossible. One might perhaps presume that TV watchers, tabloid readers, and movie goers exercise and sharpen their eyes. But the opposite is true. The ancient sages knew exactly why they called the "concupiscence of the eyes" a "destroyer". The restoration of man's inner eyes can hardly be expected in this day and age—unless, first of all, one were willing and determined simply to exclude from one's realm of life all those inane and contrived but titillating illusions incessantly generated by the entertainment industry.

You may argue, perhaps: true, our capacity to see has diminished, but such loss is merely the price all higher cultures have to pay. We have lost, no doubt, the American Indian's keen sense of smell, but we also no longer need it since we have binoculars, compass, and radar. Let me repeat: in this obviously continuing process there exists a limit below which human nature itself is threatened, and the very integrity of human existence is directly endangered. Therefore, such ultimate danger can no longer be averted with technology alone. At stake here is this: How can man be saved from becoming a totally passive consumer of mass-produced goods and a subservient follower beholden to every slogan the managers may proclaim? The question really is: How can man preserve and safeguard the foundation of his spiritual dimension and an uncorrupted relationship to reality?

The capacity to perceive the visible world "with our own eyes" is indeed an essential constituent of human nature. We are talking here about man's essential inner richness—or, should the threat prevail, man's most abject inner poverty. And why so? To *see* things is the first step toward that primordial and basic mental grasping of reality, which constitutes the essence of man as a spiritual being.

I am well aware that there are realities we can come to know through "hearing" alone. All the same, it remains a fact that only through seeing, indeed through seeing with our own eyes, is our inner autonomy established. Those no longer able to see reality with their own eyes are equally unable to hear correctly. It is specifically the man thus impoverished who inevitably falls prey to the demagogical spells of any powers that be. "Inevitably", because such a person is utterly deprived even of the potential to keep a critical distance (and here we recognize the direct political relevance of our topic).

The diagnosis is indispensable yet only a first step. What, then, may be proposed; what can be done?

We already mentioned simple abstention, a regimen of fasting and abstinence, by which we would try to keep the visual noise of daily inanities at a distance. Such an approach seems to me indeed an indispensable first step but, all the same, no more than the removal, say, of a roadblock.

A better and more immediately effective remedy is this: *to be active oneself in artistic creation, producing shapes and forms for the eye to see.*

Nobody has to observe and study the visible mystery of a human face more than the one who sets out to sculpt it in a tangible medium. And this holds true not only for a manually formed image. The verbal "image" as well can thrive only when it springs from a higher level of visual perception. We sense the intensity of observation required simply to say, "The girl's eyes were gleaming like wet currants" (Tolstoy).

Before you can express anything in tangible form, you first need eyes to see. The mere attempt, therefore, to create an artistic form compels the artist to take a fresh look at the visible reality; it requires authentic and personal observation. Long before a creation is completed, the artist has gained for himself another and more intimate achievement: a deeper and more receptive vision, a more intense awareness, a sharper and more discerning understanding, a more patient openness for all things quiet and inconspicuous, an eye for things previously overlooked. In short: the artist will be able to perceive with new eyes the abundant wealth of all visible reality, and, thus challenged, additionally acquires the inner capacity to absorb into his mind such an exceedingly rich harvest. The capacity to *see* increases.

THOUGHTS ABOUT MUSIC

P HILOSOPHERS, ESPECIALLY THOSE interested also in the practical things of culture and education, like to reflect on the essence of music, and not only because of some rather accidental and personal propensity for it. No, this special interest parallels a great tradition harking back almost to primeval times, certainly to Pythagoras, Plato, and the sages of the Far East. Not only is music one of the most amazing and mysterious phenomena of all the world's *miranda*, the things that make us wonder (and, therefore, the formal subject matter of any philosopher, as Aristotle and St. Thomas declare). Not only has it even been said, and rightly so, that music may be nothing but a secret philosophizing of the soul, an *Exercitium Metaphysice Occultum*. Yet, with the soul entirely oblivious, that philosophy, in fact, is happening here—according to Schopenhauer in his profound discourse on the metaphysics of music. Beyond that, and above all, music prompts the philosopher's continued interest because it is by its nature so *close to the fundamentals of human existence*. It is this very reason that compels all those concerned with culture and education to pay special attention to the art and the performance of music.

This address was given during intermission at a Bach concert at the *Pädagogische Akademie Essen* (Winter 1951/52); published in *Wort und Wahrheit*, May 1952.

The one question particularly intriguing to the searching mind of the philosopher when he reflects on the phenomenon of music is this: *What* indeed do we perceive when we listen to music? We obviously perceive more and something other than the specific sounds produced by the bow on the strings of a violin, by the air blown into a flute, or by the finger hitting the keys of a piano. All these sounds, of course, also reach the ears of those who cannot relate to music at all (should such a species exist). These sounds alone, no doubt, do not yet constitute music as such! What, then, do we essentially perceive when we listen to music in the proper manner?

Other forms of art provide much easier answers, even though it would also be rather difficult to answer the question, "What do we really perceive when we look at—say—Dürer's 'Detail of a Meadow'?" It is obviously not the blades of grass, which we can observe, even more realistically, also in nature or in a photograph. It is not the blades of grass, not "this particular object" at all, which in truth we see whenever we look at a painting in the proper manner. Or again: *What* indeed do we perceive when we listen to a poem, when we become aware of the poetic energy pulsating in a poem? We obviously perceive more and something other than the factual, literal meaning of its words (this direct meaning has even been called the impurity of all poetry—an *indispensable* impurity, though). Such questions, we realize, are equally difficult to answer.

But back to our initial question: *What* do we perceive when we listen to music with the "right ears"? We certainly cannot speak of any particular "object" as is found in the fine arts or poetry where perforce *something* is represented, *something* is expressed (some objective reality, for instance). Music cannot claim an object of this kind, in spite of occasional contrary opinions even on the part of great musicians. It is indeed *not* the "Idyll at the Brook", or the "Thunderstorm", or the "Happy Gathering of Countryfolk" we *really* perceive when listening to Beethoven's Sixth Symphony. But what about "songs"? Is it not, in this case at least, the meaning of the words that constitutes what we "really" perceive when an aria or song recital is offered? Of course we hear the words! And yet, provided we witness authentic and significant music and provided we listen in the proper manner, we invariably perceive an *additional*, most intimate, meaning that would be absent from the words *alone*. This "most intimate" meaning is not expressed by the words alone, whether written or spoken! *What*, then, do we perceive in music?

Music "does not speak of things but tells of weal and woe". This formulation by Schopenhauer somehow sums up the sentiments, variously stated, of many thinkers throughout the centuries. It would not be entirely correct to consider that this statement expresses the fullness of the conception found in classic Western philosophy; it at least opens an access to the main idea as it leads us in the right direction. "Weal and woe"—these are concepts related to the will; they point to the *bonum*, the good, seen as the intrinsic moving force of the will. The will is always directed toward the good.

At this point, a word of caution is in order against moralistic misconceptions. This is what we mean: man's being is always dynamic (*geschehendes Sein*); man is never just "there". Man "is" insofar as he "becomes"—not only in his physical reality, in growing, maturing, and eventually diminishing toward the end. In his spiritual reality, too, man is constantly moving on—he is existentially "becoming"; he is "on the way". For man, to "be" means to "be on the way"—he *cannot be* in any other form; man is intrinsically a pilgrim, "not yet arrived", regardless of whether he is aware of this or not, whether he accepts it or not. The object of this dynamism, the destination of this journey, the aim, therefore, of this becoming and the moving force underlying it all, is the *good*. Even when man pursues evil, he intends a perceived good. We may even say (and the great teachers in the tradition of Western wisdom *did* say it) that this unquenchable inner dynamism, this persistent restlessness at the core of the unfolding human existence, this yearning has only one objective: perfect happiness, the state of bliss (*Glückseligkeit*). Subconsciously, and apart from any specific act of the will but also in the innermost core of all our conscious exercise of the will, we yearn for perfect happiness. In *this* lies man's fulfillment, man's *good*, the beckoning aim and destiny of his unfolding existence!

The ultimate object of the human will and the process itself of *becoming*, by which we approach yet never quite reach this goal with the infinitely variable steps in countless apparent or true detours of our personal time frame: neither this object nor this process can ever be adequately described in words, neither the destination nor the journey. St. Augustine declares: "The *Good*—you hear this word and you take a deep breath; you hear it and you utter a sigh." And he adds that man is unable to put into words the central and full meaning of the concept of the *good*, its complete realization: "We cannot say, and yet cannot be silent either. . . . What are we to do, employing neither speech nor silence? We ought to rejoice! *Jubilate!* Shout out your heart's delight in wordless jubilation!" Such "wordless jubilation" (at least *one* of its manifestations) is known as *music*!

Of course, it is not always jubilation. Since the good, the goal, is not easily achieved, and since the journey can be arduous, even headed in the wrong direction, there can also be a wordless expression of sadness, of confident hope, yearning, grief, or despair. To articulate such intimate realities, the dynamism of human existence itself, the spoken word, proves utterly inadequate. Such realities, by their very nature (and also because of the spirit's nature), exist *before* as well as *beyond* all speech. "And so we see", says Kierkegaard, "that music in relation to the spoken word is both the leader and the follower, coming both first and last." Music opens a path into the realm of silence. Music reveals the human soul in stark "nakedness", as it were, *without* the customary linguistic draperies, "which usually get entangled in ever present thorns" (Paul Claudel).

To repeat: thus has the nature of music variously been understood in the Western philosophical tradition—as nonverbal articulation of weal and woe; as wordless expression of man's intrinsic dynamism of self-realization, a process understood as man's journey toward ethical personhood, as the manifestation of man's will in all its aspects, as love. This, for instance, is the meaning of Plato's statement that music "imitates the impulses of the soul", or as Aristotle puts it: music is similar to ethics and related to it. The same tradition continues in remarks by Kierkegaard, Schopenhauer, and Nietzsche when they say that music "invariably is the direct expression of an immediacy as no interfering medium is involved"; or (Schopenhauer) that of all the arts it is music that represents the *will* itself; or (Nietzsche in his interpretation of Wagner) that music lets us hear "nature transformed into love".

What is stated here in so many words simply amounts to this: music articulates the inner dynamism of man's existential self, which is music's "prime matter" (so to speak), and both share a particular characteristic—both move in *time*.

But "music" is never some impersonal, abstract energy; it is "performed" by musicians with all their distinctive individualities. Consequently, a thousand different musical expressions of that inner dynamism can appear. And since the inner growth into ethical personhood is not determined by any unchangeable law of nature but is a process shaped and threatened by countless dangers and interferences, a thousand different expressions of pretense, error, and confusion can also appear.

Thus the musical articulation may include a shallow contentment with the facile availability of the cheapest "goods", the rejection of any ordered structure, the despairing denial that man's existential becoming has a goal at all or that such a goal could be reached. There can also be, as in Thomas Mann's *Doctor Faustus*, the music of nihilism, which lives on parody and comes about through the "devil's help and hellish fire under the cauldron".

This distinct possibility of corruption, this danger ever present where music is made, was clearly seen by the sages of old, especially Plato and Aristotle, and they tried to counteract it.

For it does not mean at all that closeness to human existence, music's proper characteristic, would find expression only in this one respect: the fundamental impulses of human existence, genuine or spurious, sincere or corrupt, would find expression in the composer's relationship to his work alone, in music alone. It does not at all mean that there would be only the realm of music itself—be it great and authentic or shallow and unconvincing music—and that on the "other side", in the realm of *listening*, there would prevail a neutral relationship of attention or inattention, of applause, of acceptance or rejection. No, that closeness to human existence implies much more.

Since music articulates the immediacy of man's basic existential dynamism in an *immediate* way, the listener as well is addressed and challenged on that profound level where man's self-realization takes place. In this existential depth of the listener, far below the level of expressible judgments, there echoes — in identical immediacy — the same vibration articulated in the audible music.

We now realize why and to what extent music plays a role in man's formation and perfection — as contribution or hindrance, and both, once again, *beyond* any conscious efforts toward formation, teaching, or education. We also realize here how indispensable it is to reflect on these very direct forces and influences. Plato and Aristotle, for example, engaged in this reflection, while we ourselves find it difficult to understand why these two great Greek thinkers, in their ethical and even *political* writings, have discussed music with such seriousness and detail. Music, according to Plato, is not only a "tool to form man's character", but also an instrument "for the right ordering of society's legal structure". In the Dialogue *The Republic* we read, "They really look on music as if it were a mere amusement and think no harm can come from it." And to believe that the only thing that matters about music is the enjoyment of the listener, regardless of whether he be "ethically worthy or not", that is, whether his inner life follows the right order or not—this opinion is most emphatically called a "lie" in Plato's late work, the *Laws*. Music is not altered without affecting society's most important rules—this, so declares Plato, had already been taught by a renowned Greek theoretician of music (Damon), and he, Plato, is convinced this is true. Of course, the "legal" aspect of a society's organization is not meant here, rather the inner order as related to the achievement of the common good. Thus we find there quite serious and detailed reflections on what forms of music, or even what kinds of musical instruments, should be banned in any properly structured society. The Middle Ages as well, up to the time of Johann Sebastian Bach, used the notion of "dishonest" instruments. What matters in all this is not the specifics; much of it, of course, is simply "conditioned" by its time and place. What *does* matter, however, is to recognize at all (*and* to put in the right order!) the intimate relationship between the music made and listened to in a society on the one hand, and the inner existential condition of such a society on the other—no different today than in Plato's time!

We ourselves, however, are probably to be counted among those who, in Plato's words, see the entire realm of music as "mere amusement", while in truth that intimate relationship between music, offered or received, and inner existential ethos all the more ominously degenerates the less a proper order is attempted. The situation commonly encountered shows that not even the awareness of the possibility of such an order is present, much less a concrete notion of such an order as the ideal.

If we now look at our society, what facts do we observe, facts that should make us think? We observe how much the most trivial and "light" music, the "happy sound", has become the most common and pervasive phenomenon. By its sheer banality, this music expresses quite accurately the cheap self-deception that on the inner existential level all is fine, there is "nothing to worry about", everything is in good order, really. We observe how much attention is demanded by—and willingly given to—the rhythmic beat of a certain crude and orgiastic music, a music "for slaves" (as Aristotle puts it). Both kinds of music, the "happy sound" as well as the numbing beat, claim legitimacy as "entertainment", as means, that is, of satisfying, without success, the boredom and existential void that are caused and increased by each other and that equally have become a common and pervasive phenomenon. We further observe how music, perhaps on a formally much higher level, is frequently selected and consumed as a means of personal enchantment, of escapism, of a certain pseudo-deliverance, and as a means to achieve delight that remains merely "skin-deep" (*von aussen her*, as Rilke said). And we observe that there is music, including great music, whose character fosters all this. We finally observe that nihilistic music, a despairing parody of creation, is not only played by great artists in novels such as *Doctor Faustus* but is real, which incidentally prompted the disturbing observation equating the history of Western music with the "history of a soul's degeneration". We observe all this with great alarm, aware that music lays bare man's inner existential condition, removing veil and façade (and it *cannot* be otherwise), while this same inner condition receives from music the most direct impulses, for better or worse. We observe and ponder all this and then are moved to rejoice as we become aware again and acknowledge anew that among all the various kinds of music today *there still exists, also and especially, the music of Johann Sebastian Bach!*

Obviously, this implies a challenge to ourselves, a challenge not easily nor "automatically" satisfied. That we are willing to listen attentively to the essential message of this music and that we let this message find an echo, as if on reverberating strings, within the immediacy of our soul is decisive. This will lead to new and rekindled clarity, authenticity, and vigor of our inward existence; to dissatisfaction with entertaining but hollow achievements; and to a sober and perceptive alertness that is not distracted from the realities of actual life by the promise of easy pleasure proffered in superficial harmonies. Above all, this will guide us to turn with resolve, constancy, courage, and hope toward the one and only *Good* by whose grace our inner existential yearning finds fulfillment; the one *Good* praised and exalted particularly in Bach's music with such ever-present "wordless jubilation".

MUSIC AND SILENCE

M USIC AND SILENCE: these are two things which, according to C. S. Lewis, cannot be found in hell. We ought to be somewhat surprised when we first read the phrase: music and silence — what a strange pairing! But then the heart of the matter becomes more and more clear. Obviously, what is here meant by silence, stillness, hush, is something quite different from that malignant absence of words which already in our present common existence is a parcel of damnation. And, as far as music is concerned, it is not difficult to imagine that in the *Inferno* its place is taken by noise, "infernal noise", pandemonium. But then, almost imperceptibly, another aspect of the issue emerges, namely, that music and silence are in fact ordered toward one another in a unique way. Both noise and total silence destroy all possibility of mutual understanding, because they destroy both speaking and hearing. Did not Konrad Weiss aptly remark that it is precisely in the midst of an age of loudness that an unbounded muteness can reign? In the same way, to the extent that it is more than mere entertainment of intoxicating rhythmic noise, music is alone in creating a particular kind of silence, though by no means soundlessly. . . . It makes a listening silence possible, but a silence that listens to more than simply sound and melody. (As a basic condition, anyone must be quiet who wants to perceive sound, whether the patient's heart-beat or a human word.) Far beyond this, music opens up a great, perfectly dimensioned space of silence within which, when things come about happily, a reality can dawn which ranks higher than music.

THREE TALKS
IN A SCULPTOR'S STUDIO

Remembrance: Mother of the Muses

IN CONVERSATIONS WITH OUR FRIEND, the lady sculptor working in this studio, there comes up every now and then the ancient Greek idea that Mnemosyne, goddess of memory, is the mother of the Muses.

But if we take a closer look at the pertinent mythological data we find several versions displaying, at first, surprising differences. All of them, as it turns out however, speak of the inner connection of the Muses with "remembrance".

The earliest and best known account goes back to the poet Hesiod, around 700 B.C.: Kronion, we read, fathered Mnemosyne's nine daughters, the Muses. A century afterward, Sappho raises her poetic voice and shows us a new aspect of the story. There is, she says, no remembrance without the Muses—obviously meaning that the Muses, on their part, inherited from their mother the unique power we call "remembrance". And again one hundred years later the hymnic poet Pindar gives still another account of how the

Birthday address, 1975; published in revised form as preface to an album by Herbert Zink, *Hilde Schürk-Frisch* (Recklinghausen: Aurel Bongers, 1980).

Muses were born: the greatest of the gods, Zeus, had ordered the chaos of the world into the harmony of the cosmos, and all the other gods beheld in admiration the splendor before their eyes. After some time Zeus asked them whether they could think of anything missing. A long silence ensues. Finally, they answer: yes, something is missing; an appropriate voice is missing to praise this creation. And for this very purpose the Muses are brought into being; it is their task to sing the praises of all creation.

These three stories about the Muses, so dissimilar at first sight, share a common, though hidden, dimension. To find out, we only have to take a closer look at the concept of "remembrance", (*Erinnerung*), which is not as clear-cut as we might have expected. "To remember" (*sich erinnern*) and "to make someone else remember" (*einen anderen erinnern*) are obviously two entirely different events. The English language, with good reason, employs two very specific verbs, "to remember" and "to remind".

The Muses, indeed, no matter how engimatic their meaning remains for us, are certainly not to be seen as beings who "remember". Rather, they help someone else to "remember"; namely, the artist, who then is not only enabled himself to remember but to help others to remember as well. If

you ask, then, what this might be which thus is re-
membered, we offer as a first reply the rather obvious reflection that the one who remembers and
the one who is helped to remember both direct
their attention away from the "here and now" and
the mere eye-catching surface. And yet, on the
other hand, the reality they now behold cannot be
something totally new either, something they
have never perceived before. It need be something
already experienced, already encountered, something that indeed no longer is part of the mind's
actual and present perception and yet stands ready
to be retrieved from memory. This, too, is so
very obvious that nobody would use the term
"remembrance" for anything other than this. So:
the one who remembers as well as the one who is
helped to remember, though not perceiving
things totally alien to him, nevertheless beholds a
"different" reality, "distinct" from his daily and
direct experience.

But now, once again, the question: What, more
specifically, is the nature of this "different" reality
that appears to our consciousness through the
power of the Muses to bring about remembrance?
Answer: though we do not see the Muses as some
sort of divine beings — of course not! — we still understand them as a real yet empirically and psy-
chologically elusive potency that brings about

inspiration. Consequently, this "different" reality can in no way be something accidental and inconsequential. It will rather be something that all too readily is ignored and "lost"—precisely because it is "different"—yet must not be forgotten if our existence is to remain truly human.

There are, indeed, large areas of reality in danger of being thus forgotten. And, of course, it is not up to the fine arts alone to counteract this danger that threatens the entire breadth and depth of human existence. Here we somehow sense the artist's inner relationship to the priest, who is called, above all, to keep alive the remembrance of a face that our intuition just barely perceives behind all immediate and tangible reality—the face of the God-man, bearing the marks of a shameful execution. Incidentally, none other than Goethe declared that the artist should be seen "as someone called to be the custodian and eager herald of an avowed sacred reality".

And yet, the artist himself, situated as he is at the center of what the Muses bring about—the process of remembrance in all its aspects: as reminder, as recollection, and as objective reality—this artist, when true to his vocation, is threatened the most. He is by nature exposed to countless possibilities of losing direction and aim. He is, above all, ever in danger of deceiving himself or—and this is not always subconsciously—deceiving others. All this is simply part and parcel of any artistic endeavor. Such perils, no doubt, can be overcome but never entirely avoided.

The artist may perchance be tempted—all the more so, the more he has acquired and mastered the "creative" possibilities of his craft—to produce an *opus* decidedly "different" from the accustomed and everyday experience of reality, yet in essence false, and in its banality a mere ruse. As is well known, fabrications of such a sort are quite assured of the public's applause.

Thomas Mann, in his *Doctor Faustus*, has fashioned a nightmare that can serve as an appropriate, though extreme, paradigm: the demonic Tempter strikes a deal with the nihilistic protagonist who craves immediate success and universal acclaim by any possible means. The deal concerns "art", created with uncommon technical skill yet entirely without substance, thriving only on the surprise it elicits by being outrageously novel and therefore unable to radiate any deeper meaning. As the Far Eastern proverb puts it, "Those who only look at themselves do ever radiate nothing." Such a product, above all, contains no remembrance nor any power to elicit remembrance, and thus has nothing to do with the Muses.

The artist who, in contrast, seeks nothing for himself, who rather keeps the recesses of his soul in silence and simplicity, receptive to the breath of creative inspiration, which then flows, by way of his own remembrance, unadulterated into the unfolding form of his work—this artist, then, may just perchance create a statue such as the "Young Woman Reclining". The statue is compellingly original, not at all a mere photographic description, because it is entirely "different" from our everyday reality. And yet, it prompts those beholding it to recall their own remembrance of the primordial archetypes veiled in this same reality. It sings the praises of creation, its poetic power bespeaks the kiss of the Muses, it touches the heart like a stanza from the Song of Songs.

Those "Guests at the Festival"

"What good are poets in barren times?" We are somewhat astonished to find, embedded in Hölderlin's great and sublime poem, "Bread and Wine", this harsh question, obviously uttered in profound disillusionment; it comes entirely unexpectedly.

Birthday address (1980).

Had it not begun with untainted and peaceful images? With the evocation of an idyllic, idealized, almost unreal past?

All around the tired town now rests,
And silence slowly fills the dim-lit alleys . . .
The market is empty of grapes and flowers . . .
No noisy hands, no hustle any more . . .
And yet, the breeze brings, softly, melodies,
The chords of lyres plucked in distant
    gardens . . ."

(Ringsum ruhet die Stadt
Still wird die erleuchtete Gasse . . .
Leer steht von Trauben und Blumen . . .
und von Werken der Hand ruht der geschäftige
    Markt . . .
Aber das Saitenspiel tönt fern aus Gärten . . .)

This is the tone throughout the opening stanza, through eighteen extended lines, in verses of immaculate and ever so vulnerable poetic beauty. And then, suddenly, though not altogether without foreboding, the desperate cry, "What good are poets in barren times!"

It seems to me worthwhile to take a moment for a closer look at this line; it offers several aspects for reflection since it is by no means as obvious as may appear at first. It does not, for instance, mean only the poet or poetry; it speaks of all artistic endeavors, including music and dance, all the fine arts in general. They would make no sense, there would be no room for them "in barren times"— this is the contention. For it is obviously not intended as a genuine question. No, it expresses a conviction, an assessment—and we immediately suspect it to be correct, disturbingly so, at least in part.

But then, what does in "barren times" mean more specifically? Barren in what respect? Hölderlin's answer is crystal clear and to the point: "barren" here means "unable to celebrate a feast"! Man's true existential lack would be his inability to celebrate a feast in a truly festive fashion. To do just this requires, as everybody knows, that the reality of our life and our world be first wholeheartedly accepted and that this acceptance, then, on special occasions, be expressed and lived out in exceptional ritual: this indeed is what it means to "celebrate a feast"! Still, at closer scrutiny, Hölderlin states something much more radical. He speaks of cultic praise and divine worship, the highest possible expression of man's acceptance of reality. It is precisely and in truth this dimension that indicates the *radix*, the root, of all festive celebration, and thus points as well to the root cause for those lamented "barren times".

Of course, someone could question here whether it is really necessary to "dig so deep", to bring in metaphysics and theology merely to explain such a simple matter as a feast. To celebrate a birthday, would we really have to affirm and accept first wholeheartedly the world in general and human existence as such? I truly believe we must, and moreover, that we probably have already done so either subconsciously or even consciously. In any event, nobody would be in a position to celebrate with gusto any birthday, neither his own nor that of a friend, should he honestly hold, with Jean Paul Sarte, that it is absurd to be born and to exist!

Any feast, not only the lofty and infrequent feast, draws its life from an attitude of acceptance, of approval, yes, of love—to use a rather high-sounding word. If this attitude is missing (and here we are again reminded of the line by Hölderlin, quoted above), if the disposition of acceptance and love is absent, not only can there be no feast, but no song either! *C'est l'amour qui chante*, love alone knows how to sing. The term "song", of course, is used here in an all-encompassing sense, including all the areas of the fine arts: poetry, music, dance, and sculpture. This is precisely the point where the intricate connection between fine arts and festival becomes evident. Both build on a loving acceptance of the world and of human existence.

It is true, I have been encouraged, in the most diplomatic manner imaginable, not to delve too deeply this time into the classics of Greek antiquity. But now, nevertheless, I have arrived, admittedly on a tricky round-about path, at a junction where I am compelled to mention the Muses, though from a somewhat surprising angle that in any event is seldom considered. Plato, calling the cultic feast a "god-given respite" from everyday drudgery, says in the same statement that we are given the Muses as guests at every festival. With this, Hölderlin's lament suddenly appears in a new light and leads directly to the obvious consequence: what good are guests coming for a festival, when there is no festival!

But if feasts are still celebrated, in spite of it all, and because feasts are still celebrated, not least in a religious context, which really is the bedrock of all festive celebration, then and therefore we need those "guests at the festival", the Muses. We need all the fine arts there. Otherwise, how could we possibly have a true celebration? A feast without song and music, without the visible form and structure of a ritual, without imagery and symbol—such a thing simply cannot even be conceived. Friedrich Schleiermacher, the theologian and translator of Plato, once stated, "The emergence of any festive reality is made possible only through the arts."

You have only to look around here, walk through the studio and the garden, and you will see everywhere how the skill of an expert artist, by many sculptures, has allowed the festive side of the world and existence to "emerge" and become visible. All these entirely earthly and realistic forms—children, young girls, loving couples, then figures of the equally earthly Sacred Story, including the Passion Story—all these forms are by no means mere copies of reality, much less aesthetic idealizations. They contain nothing false. And yet, they reside nonetheless outside the common reality of everyday life—and thus, through the magic of artistic transfiguration, make us perceive, if ever so vaguely, the paradise of uncorrupted primordial forms beneath the obvious surface of that still discernible common reality. And herein precisely consists the festive character of any feast: in being at the same time the remembrance of primordial bliss and the anticipation of future fulfillment, it is both. I used the term "paradise". This word does indeed and equally indicate both the as yet uncorrupted original reality and the once again healed and healing condition of the realm beyond death. And neither can be captured by idealizing and innocuous pleasantries! In the same way, to "celebrate a feast" cannot simply be equated with merrymaking. Being joyful — yes, indeed! But then:

> They tried, yet in vain, to tell me
> Of joy in words sounding joyful —
> Here am I taught, at last,
> Here, in this sadness-filled tale.

> (Manche versuchten umsonst,
> das Freudigste freudig zu sagen.
> Hier spricht endlich es mir,
> hier in der Trauer sich aus.)

So, once again, says Hölderlin (in a distich on *Antigone*, the classical Greek tragedy).

The dimension of "paradise", in any case, remains a valid attribute. All that exists carries somehow the imprint of "paradise", and all authentic fine arts, offspring of the Muses, know how to make this truth transparent. If you, inside this atelier, contemplate in true meditation the most moving and affecting image of the "Last Conversation" between two crucified victims, you will surely remember the central word in that conversation, the closing word: paradise.

It is a marvelous talent, though — as I well know — not easy to bear, that is thus empowered to hold up before our mental and physical eyes the festive and paradise-evoking aspect of creation, be ours a "barren time" or not.

Vita contemplativa—The Contemplative Life

I come here as a guest, kindly received and connected to you in friendship, not really endowed with great expertise in art (some have declared me entirely devoid of any), yet claiming a somewhat philosophical and reflective mind. As such I have had the opportunity for several decades now to follow and observe closely what was going on and happening in this studio. Today I wish to express as best I can how I perceive the artistic work of our mutual friend—what makes it unique and what distinguishes it from so many things that dominate the contemporary art scene.

The distinguishing and characterizing element in the artistic creativity we celebrate today lies, as I am convinced, in this: we witness an expression of the contemplative life, the *vita contemplativa*.

Birthday address (1985); published in *Hirschberg* 38 (1985) under the title, "Zum 70. Geburtstag von Hilde Schürk-Frisch".

This at first sounds surprising if not outright unbelievable to anybody who has ever observed, maybe many times, how great a manual exertion is required, up to the limits of physical endurance (and sometimes beyond), to bring about the plaster or clay model of a particular sculpture. All the same, I still say: the beginning of it all is contemplation!

This concept can hardly be explained in a brief definition. Its immediate and direct meaning indicates seeing, beholding, perceiving some reality. Incidentally, you may find it astonishing how much and how unanimously the great thinkers of the Western tradition have extolled that attitude of receptive observation. The earliest statement, one hundred years before Plato, comes to us from the city of Athens, from Anaxagoras, who to the catechism-like question, "Why are you here on earth?" replied, "To behold"—*eis theorian* (a Greek expression, later translated by the Romans as *contemplatio*!). And from Anaxagoras we can go to Goethe and Teilhard de Chardin. In Goethe's *Wahlverwandtschaften* (*Elective Affinities*) we read: "Our self-awareness is always connected to seeing. I believe our dreams have only one purpose: that our seeing may not be interrupted." Teilhard de Chardin prefaces his major work on the *Phenomenon of Man* with a rather strange and seemingly unrelated prologue. He states that all life is contained in the act of seeing, and that the entire evolution of the universe has as its final aim nothing else but the bringing forth of ever more perfect eyes. So, once again: to contemplate means first of all *to see*—and not *to think*!

In the entire work of our sculptor friend you will not encounter anything not truly resulting from seeing; none of it is born of mere thinking or reasoning, much less is it arbitrarily contrived. Here precisely lies for me the decisive distinction and difference: there is nothing here even remotely resembling those "objects" that regularly dominate certain art exhibitions, the ones labeled by Eugène Ionesco, a few years ago, "storage rooms" and "museums of our despair".

The true artist, however, is not someone who simply and in any way whatever "sees" things. So that he can create form and image (not only in bronze and stone but through word and speech as well), he must be endowed with the ability to see in an exceptionally *intensive* manner. The concept of contemplation also contains this special intensified way of seeing. A twofold meaning is hereby intended: the gift of retaining and preserving in one's own memory whatever has been visually perceived. How meticulously, how intensively—with the heart, as it were—must a sculptor have gazed on a human face before being able, as is our friend here, to render a portrait, as if by magic, entirely from memory! And this is our second point: to *see* in contemplation, moreover, is not limited only to the tangible surface of reality; it certainly perceives more than mere appearances. Art flowing from contemplation does not so much attempt to copy reality as rather to capture the *archetypes* of all that is. Such art does not want to depict what everybody already sees but to make visible what not everybody sees.

If we now look from this perspective at the artistic work before us, we clearly see an art that is *neither-nor*: *neither* is it "abstract", much less "absolute" art, which is indifferent to the forms of the visible world; *nor* can we speak of a blunt and merely descriptive realism. These two somewhat involuted opposites need an explanation; after all, what do we mean by "neither realism nor abstraction"? To this end we have to consider a certain aspect of the term "contemplation", so far not yet mentioned. For even the most intensive seeing and beholding may not yet be true contemplation. Rather, the ancient expression of the mystics applies here: *ubi amor, ibi oculus*—the eyes see better when guided by love; a new dimension of "seeing" is opened up by love alone! And this means contemplation is visual perception prompted by loving acceptance!

I hold that this is the specific mark of seeing things in contemplation: it is motivated by loving acceptance, by an affectionate affirmation. Nothing would be more alien to our sculptor friend and her work than to revile, despise, and distort reality, or explicitly to destroy all ordered form — not at all a rare phenomenon nowadays. Not only her madonnas, her portraits, her statues of children, her "Girl with a Ginkgo Leaf" — not only these but even the tortured and contorted face of the crucified thief, his mouth gaping in a last cry for help — even this proclaims an affectionate devotion to mankind and all things created.

And yet, nothing in this affirming closeness to reality smacks of false idealization, nothing is embellished as if all reality were wholesome and without rough edges — not even in those instances when her statues succeed in embodying "beauty" itself. Once again, this too is the result of a certain characteristic of seeing things in loving contemplation. This characteristic is difficult to define, and I am not at all certain I can find the right words. Yet I shall try. The German language, in its vocabulary concerning loving attitudes, uses the rather curious expression, *sich nicht satt sehen können* ("can't see enough" of something), which, indeed, has a twofold meaning. In one respect, it indicates utmost delight; thus new parents "can't see enough" of their baby. But then it also means that the desire to "see enough" is never satisfied. In this craving to "see" there is a dimension that— as a matter of fact, even of necessity—*always* remains unfulfilled! Decisive here is whether an artist experiences and accepts this. Those in the fine arts who all too hastily have "seen enough"; that is, those who are satisfied with the outward appearance of things, may easily be content with contriving some smooth and crowd-pleasing yet shallow fabrication. Those, however, who have—perhaps painfully—experienced and accepted, even in the delight of their beholding eyes, that ultimately their longing will not and cannot be fulfilled, those will be unable to create mere pleasing, agreeable, frictionless art. Konrad Weiss once remarked, "Contemplation will not be satisfied until blinded by the object of its ultimate desires." Such a statement almost leads us beyond the confines of this world.